DSC SPEED READS
MANAGEMENT

Decision-making

Debra Allcock Tyler

Published by the Directory of Social Change (Registered Charity no. 800517 in England and Wales)

Registered address: Directory of Social Change, First Floor, 10 Queen Street Place, London EC4R 1BE

Tel: 020 4526 5995

Visit www.dsc.org.uk to find out more about our books, subscription funding website and training events. You can also sign up for e-newsletters so that you're always the first to hear about what's new.

The publisher welcomes suggestions and comments that will help to inform and improve future versions of this and all of our titles. Please give us your feedback by emailing publications@dsc.org.uk.

It should be understood that this publication is intended for guidance only and is not a substitute for professional advice. No responsibility for loss occasioned as a result of any person acting or refraining from acting can be accepted by the author or publisher.

Print and digital editions first published 2024

Copyright © Directory of Social Change 2024

All rights reserved. No part of the printed version of this book may be stored in a retrieval system or reproduced in any form whatsoever without prior permission in writing from the publisher. This book is sold subject to the condition that it shall not, by way of trade or otherwise, be lent, re-sold, hired out or otherwise circulated without the publisher's prior permission in any form of binding or cover other than that in which it is published, and without a similar condition including this condition being imposed on the subsequent purchaser.

The digital version of this publication may only be stored in a retrieval system for personal use. No part may be edited, amended, extracted or reproduced in any form whatsoever. It may not be distributed or made available to others without prior permission in writing from the publisher.

The publisher and author have made every effort to contact copyright holders. If anyone believes that their copyright material has not been correctly acknowledged, please contact the publisher, who will be pleased to rectify the omission.

The moral right of the author has been asserted in accordance with the Copyrights, Designs and Patents Act 1988.

ISBN 978 1 78482 105 0 (print edition)
ISBN 978 1 78482 106 7 (digital edition)

British Library Cataloguing in Publication Data
A catalogue record for this book is available from the British Library

Cover and text design by Kate Griffith
Printed and bound in the UK by Martins the Printers, Berwick upon Tweed

Contents

Introduction — 4

Chapter 1: What are you trying to achieve? — 5
- What is a decision? — 5
- Bad decision-making — 6
- Questions to consider — 6

Chapter 2: The psychological factors — 12
- Time — 12
- Experience — 13
- The messenger — 14
- Risk appetite — 15
- Ego — 17
- Framing — 18

Chapter 3: Building up to the decision point — 19
- Gathering information — 19
- Consultation — 20
- The process of decision-making — 23

Chapter 4: Implementing the decision — 26
- Brief — 26
- Implement — 27
- Check — 28
- Amend — 29

Chapter 5: Following up — 30
- Why evaluate? — 30
- Evaluate — 31
- Remember — 32

Introduction

Who will this book help?

This guide is for anyone who is involved in decision-making at any level of an organisation. This includes trustees, the executive team, other staff and volunteers. The more senior in your organisation you find yourself, the more likely you are to be tasked with decision-making; however, the principles in this book will be helpful at any stage of your career.

What will it give you?

This book will help you to understand whether a decision is truly needed, establish what the decision is meant to achieve, recognise what factors influence the quality of the decision, and outline the key actions to take in making the decision, implementing it and learning from it. It will also help you to understand the processes and dynamics of decision-making, and to determine who is best placed to make decisions and in which context.

Chapter 1

What are you trying to achieve?

This chapter explores what decision-making is and the sorts of decision you might face.

What is a decision?

This sounds like a really daft question, right? But it's a pretty important one, because there are so many different kinds of decision that we make all the time, both conscious and unconscious. A decision is basically making a choice about something to do (action) or some way of thinking (belief). Such as deciding to buy potatoes rather than carrots (action) or that you no longer believe in the Tooth Fairy (belief). Decisions can be very specific to your domestic and personal sphere (such as choosing a paint colour for your kitchen) or further-reaching (such as implementing a new operational structure at work or choosing how to vote in an election). We make thousands of decisions every day (even if that decision is not to make one!). Unconsciously, we decide to scratch our nose, wiggle our toes or sneeze. Consciously, we decide what to wear, what to eat, what task to do next and so on. Our brains are a constant decision-making mechanism, and most decisions are quick, relatively easy and not very risky.

The challenge comes when the decisions we need to take are more complex and important, where less information than we need is available to us and where the consequences of those decisions are potentially risky. That's when we can either freeze into inaction or rush into a hurried decision and risk it turning out to be 'bad'.

Bad decision-making

In reality, of course, there is rarely such a thing as an objectively bad decision. It's highly unusual to be presented in advance with a clear and binary 'this decision is good; that decision is bad' set of options. Most decisions are realised as good or bad only in hindsight with the aid of the infallible 'retrospectroscope' – and many land somewhere in between. Also, decisions that appear to be good to one person may seem ridiculous to another, so subjectivity is always at play. We make choices based on the information available to us at the time, maximising our knowledge and experience, and with the best of faith and good intent.

> **Top tip**
>
> 'It's not about making the right decision – it's about making the decision right.'
>
> **Vicky Browning, former CEO, ACEVO**

If you have taken a decision that turns out to not deliver what you hoped for, you can track back and review if you missed anything during your decision-making process that you can improve the next time. But there is no point beating yourself or anyone else up if it turned out to be a bad decision. If you'd known that at the time, you would have taken a different one – so give yourself and others a break!

Questions to consider

To make a decision, very simply, you need to begin by asking yourself a number of questions.

Why is this a decision?

This is quite a key question. Some decisions don't need to be made or, at the very least, are better delayed. However, it is important to be clear that the decision is to *delay* the decision – not to just leave folk hanging.

Decisions are typically taken to solve problems or to move something forward. It won't be a good decision if you're not clear exactly what the problem is or what you want to be different as a result of the decision. For example, if you're struggling with staff retention, you might assume the problem is with the pay you offer and increase salaries, creating a potentially unaffordable cost in the long term. In fact, poor staff retention might be related to people having to commute to the office and higher pay won't make much of a difference. You might decide to introduce remote working instead. Or if it's about people not feeling valued, you might bring in appropriate training for your managers.

You need to ask yourself if it actually needs to be a decision at all. Could this be something that you simply allow to evolve or develop, giving time for other information to come to light, without going through a process of decision-making? For example, a charity supporting refugees and planning a marketing campaign might decide to wait for a decision on a government policy, a new piece of legislation or a change in regulations that might affect its beneficiaries before going ahead with the campaign.

Similarly, if you are considering a merger or a collaboration with another organisation, you might wait for its latest financial data to become available or for circumstances in the overall external economy to become clearer before deciding. Or if you are considering a restructure and know or suspect that some people might be retiring or leaving the organisation, it can be prudent to see how things pan out naturally before rushing a decision.

What sort of decision is it?

Another key question. There are three core types of decision and a fourth that I would like you to consider at the end of this section.

Authoritarian. This is a decision that is made by one person, whether that is a senior executive or any staff member dealing with the situation. They may well listen to others' views, but ultimately it is for them to decide what course of action to take. This approach can be very quick but harder to implement. That is because, although there are some folk who like being told what to do, many may resist it.

Unanimous or consensus. These two types both require you to persuade everyone to agree, otherwise the decision can't be implemented. They have the benefit of having everyone on board. However, making a decision can take a long time, and you run the risk of watering down a good proposal because you have to get everyone to agree. I'm not a fan of these types of decision, mainly because I've seen charities compromise to the extent that big, bold, brave things don't happen, as you're trying to keep everyone happy. Another risk with these approaches is that folk may go along with the prevalent view just for a quiet life. An example is deciding on where to go on holiday with your family. One of you wants to go to explore the volcanoes in Iceland, the others want to go to Ibiza to sunbathe and party. You end up in Scotland as that's the only place that everyone can agree on. Not that Scotland isn't a lovely place to holiday! But in this case, it doesn't really satisfy anyone.

Majority. This is where you get folk to argue for one side or the other and then vote on which argument won. The benefit is that it feels democratic, and the losers just have to suck up the majority decision. However, getting to a majority vote can be a lengthy process. Sometimes debate can be quite heated, quieter voices aren't heard and you also run the risk that the minority view isn't given fair representation. Just like with the consensus or unanimous approaches above, people might give in to persuasive loud voices just to avoid arguments. Also, those who voted against a decision then find it very hard to back down and are more inclined to look for flaws as the decision is being implemented.

Alignment. There is a slightly different approach to getting to a decision which I encourage. And that's to go with alignment rather than getting folk to agree or disagree. When you ask people to change their position from disagree to agree, you are in effect asking them to say their view is wrong. That is incredibly hard for human beings to do. Instead, try asking people if they can align behind a decision, not necessarily agree with it. In this scenario, you're not asking folk to say they were wrong, but you are allowing them the space to say 'Yes, OK, I can get behind this, despite my reservations.' It really helps to reduce conflict and allows folk to share their disagreement, but it gets rid of that win/lose paradigm. It's not foolproof, of course, but it does usually make decision-making a bit easier.

How important is the decision?

Is this decision going to profoundly change the way you do something, or have a big impact on a human being or beings? Or is it something relatively small that doesn't matter that much? Is it something that might seem small at the time but have huge ramifications in the future?

It is important to understand what level of impact the decision will have – and to really think it through. Remember that what doesn't seem a big deal to you might feel significant to someone else. Who is going to be affected by it and in what way? A small change like bringing forward a meeting time might have a big impact on someone juggling childcare or caring responsibilities, for example. Consider checking in with others even if the issue feels minor to you.

When does it need to be taken by?

Is the decision urgent or immediate? Is it something that you need to decide now or later? Think about the consequences of delaying it and the consequences of taking it too quickly.

Timing can be quite important here. Is there an optimum time for the decision to be made? For example, if you're thinking about a restructure, it might be better delayed until the start of a new financial year when you have your financial plans in place. Or, alternatively, it might be better towards the end of the old financial year so that people start the new year with the new structure.

Whose job is it to take the decision?

This is often the source of conflict in charities – especially when deciding whether the decision is best made by the board of trustees or the executive team, or someone down the line. My rule of thumb is: the further up the management chain you are, the fewer decisions you should be taking. Most decisions should be taken at the point where the action is delivered. The board of trustees should be making very few decisions – and certainly not operational ones. Board-level decisions should mostly be about strategy, top-level budgets and values. They are about setting the parameters within which other people can take the decisions that deliver the strategy, the budget or the values. Everything else is operational-level stuff and should be left to the executive team and other staff.

> ### Case study – Taking decisions at the wrong level
> The trustees of a charity decided that they didn't like the leadership structure in the organisation. They forced the CEO to change it to what they thought the structure should be, including appointing a new director of strategy. To make matters worse, the trustees insisted on being part of the recruitment panel.
>
> You will be unsurprised to hear it went horribly wrong. The leadership team resisted the new structure, some folk got promoted and others demoted, the CEO's heart wasn't in it, because he knew this was the wrong approach and that folk were in the wrong jobs, and everyone resented the new director of strategy.
>
> When the proverbial hit the fan, the CEO couldn't be held to account, and the trustees were (rightly) blamed – after all, it had been their decision, against the CEO's advice. The trustees had forgotten that delivering the work of the charity is the CEO's job and that it includes how the organisation is structured. It's OK for trustees to give their advice, if asked, but not to make the decision.

When boards interfere with operational and delivery decisions, it often goes horribly wrong. Of course, in very small charities, trustees are not just the strategists but also the doers. In such cases, when making a decision, you need to be clear in which capacity you are acting. Are you deciding as a trustee thinking about the future of the charity or are you deciding as a volunteer concerned with the immediate impact on beneficiaries?

> ### Decision-making at board level
> Board-level decisions should largely be restricted to agreeing the following:
> - The vision and direction of the charity
> - The annual budget
> - Any major plans that take up a lot of time and resource
> - Any out-of-budget expenditure
> - High-level policies, in particular those that implement law or regulatory requirements such as discipline
> - The overall salary budget
> - The reserves policy
> - The risk appetite
> - Special strategic projects
> - Appointing new trustees
> - Appointing the CEO
> - The remuneration package of the CEO
> - Departures to or variations on all the above!
>
> From Debra Allcock-Tyler, *It's a Battle on the Board,* London, Directory of Social Change, 2020, p. 162.

Chapter 2

The psychological factors

This chapter looks at the ways in which your thinking can interfere with your ability to make informed and effective decisions.

Decision-making can appear relatively simple. You have a decision to make, you gather information in order to make that decision, you weigh up the pros and cons, and then you make it. Ah, I wish it was that easy! The reality is that there is a whole lot of stuff going on in our brains that interferes with what we think ought to be a straightforward process. It is incredibly important to be aware of all of the psychological factors that might influence your decision-making so that you don't fall prey to them. These factors can be broadly grouped into six main areas: time, experience, the messenger, risk appetite, ego and framing.

Time

The amount of time you have to make a decision will inevitably affect the quality of the decision – although more time does not necessarily make for better decisions. If you have too much time, you can sometimes also accrue too much information and so run the risk of being overwhelmed by detail and unable to see the bigger picture. If you have very little time, and therefore probably not enough time to gather the best information, you run the risk of making a hasty decision without having thought it all through.

There is no perfect amount of time, of course – you only know that in hindsight – but you can decide on the right amount of time depending on the impact of the decision. If it's a big one about the strategic direction of your organisation, which will have a significant impact on its work in the long term, then you need to give yourself a reasonable amount of time to gather information and debate options. It's also important to make sure you're not pressured into making a quick call in such situations.

If it's a small decision where the impact is minimal, then don't use precious time gathering information which probably won't make much difference.

Experience

None of us exist in a vacuum. We carry with us all of our experience thus far, both conscious and unconscious, and we bring that experience to bear when making decisions. The problem is that our experiences are fixed, and that can mean that we don't always approach decisions with an open mind.

Another issue is that they are *our* experiences, and others will have different ones – you are in danger of ending up in an argument about whose experience is more valid.

This also links with the availability heuristic (a heuristic is basically a 'rule of thumb', something we have learned to use as a shortcut in our thinking). This heuristic means that we make decisions about a thing based on the most recent experience we have of a similar thing. For example, if we ate a dodgy prawn, we might decide all prawns make us sick even though that might have been a one-off incident.

We tend to overemphasise those things that we can readily call to mind – either because they happened very recently or because they had some kind of an emotional impact on us at the time. This means that we are more likely to overestimate the probability of a similar thing happening, even in a new situation.

> ### Case study – Deciding from fear
>
> A charity once acquired another organisation, thinking it was the right decision, and it went disastrously wrong, costing a huge amount of money in legal fees and compensation.
>
> Some time afterwards, the opportunity arose to take over a much smaller charity. The risks were absolutely minimal, and the long-term benefits could have been substantial. However, the trustees were so burned by the failure of the previous acquisition that they rejected the proposal out of hand. Their decision was not based on calm logic but on fear.
>
> The charity they rejected then merged with another organisation – and that proved to be hugely successful. An opportunity lost because of fear based on a previous experience.

So, it's important to ask openly – are you making the decision to reject this particular idea or proposal because of something that happened in the past and not because you are calmly looking at it on its own merits? Is it really the same or likely to have the same outcome?

The messenger

How we feel about someone influences how seriously we take the information that they are providing. We can conflate the messenger of the idea or information with what we think about them as a person. And this is often emotionally driven. If we don't like someone much, we are less likely to take their input as positively as we will if it's someone we like. You see this in public life a lot. If someone likes a politician, there's pretty much nothing that you can say that will influence their view on what that politician says. Ditto if you dislike them – you will dismiss everything they say.

> **Top tip**
> Ask yourself if you would have the same reaction if the information was being given by someone else.

The same happens in the workplace. Trustees or colleagues you're not so fond of and trust less are unlikely to seem as credible to you as those whom you really admire and trust.

Your feelings about someone should not influence your assessment of the facts or information – or even view or opinion – that they are giving to you. So it's important to challenge your reaction to the input you are getting. Are you sure you are listening to the information and not judging it – either positively or negatively – based on what you think of the individual or indeed their motives?

Risk appetite

Your ability to take big decisions will be highly influenced by how courageous you are about risk.

Studies by psychologists (Daniel Kahneman in particular) show that humans are very often driven by what is called 'loss aversion'. That is, we are more afraid of losing something than of gaining something else. So we tend to emphasise losses over gains. Even if the gain is potentially huge, if we feel that we might lose something, it constrains our ability to take bigger risks. This is an emotional reaction, not a logical one.

> **Where next?**
> I strongly recommend reading *Thinking, Fast and Slow* by Daniel Kahneman. It talks about the two key drivers of thinking and decision-making: System 1 (being fast, instinctive and emotional) and System 2 (being slower and more logic based). Both are valid, of course, but the book outlines how they each can influence our decisions.

You need to consider what you are reacting to in terms of risk. Are you trying to avoid risk altogether? (Pretty impossible, to be honest – every decision comes with some level of risk.) Are you overemphasising what could go wrong and forgetting about the outcome you want to achieve? Are you more afraid of what you might lose than what you might gain? Have you weighed up the benefits you will get against what you might lose and apportioned the proper value to them?

> ### Case study – Taking the risk
> A friend of mine was a highly paid banker – and utterly miserable in his job. His relationships were suffering, he was stressed, unhealthy and unhappy. But he and his family lived a very nice life in terms of material things.
>
> So the risk of handing in his notice and leaving was huge: a big financial hit to him and his family. No more foreign holidays, no new cars, no more eating out a few times a week, no more expensive gifts on birthdays, less financial support for his kids at university, who would have to work to help pay for their food and accommodation – basically, everything would be downgraded. And he wouldn't be able to provide for his family all he had aspired to.
>
> He and his family had to take all of this into account when deciding what he should do. And they had to weigh up his physical and mental health against what they would lose materially.
>
> In the end, he did leave and is now a supermarket delivery driver. He has never been happier. They are managing fine on a much reduced income, he is much fitter, he has a better-quality relationship with his family, he is working fewer hours and only those he chooses to, he has more time with the family and his dogs to take long walks or relax at home. Everyone is in a much better place.

Ego

Human beings are social animals. We need to feel a sense of belonging. We need to feel accepted and valued by our peers. We are very driven by how we want others to see us and how we fit in with our social groups. That's how society thrives, of course! The downside is that sometimes our desire to fit in can overcome our judgement about a particular decision or even our willingness to challenge or put forward an alternative perspective.

I remember a situation where a trustee had asked the executive team to put forward a proposal to the rest of the board of trustees about working with another charity. She even worked with the executive team on the proposal. When the proposal was put to the vote, it was rejected – even by the trustee who had helped to design it. When the executive team asked the trustee about her decision afterwards, she said she didn't want to look as if she was siding with the executive team against the rest of the board of trustees. This is a prime example of wanting to fit in with a group, despite your own personal views. We want to be admired and liked by our peers and those we lead. That's perfectly understandable. But we must be alive to the possibility that that desire might get in the way of good decision-making.

This is especially challenging at board level, where trustees don't know each other that well. They don't meet very often and haven't had the chance to build the types of trusting relationship you get in a team you work with all the time, so they are less likely to challenge the status quo or offer contrary evidence.

A good way to reduce the impact our natural desire to fit in has on decision-making is to frame any discussion question in such a way that no one feels they are being forced to 'take sides' against another colleague. For example:

- Does anyone have any contrary points to this?
- Is anyone aware of any examples of someone who's done this before and succeeded/failed?

- Is anyone prepared to play Devil's Advocate on this?

Or even something as simple as 'let's list the pros and cons'.

Framing

Framing is another factor that can influence our decisions. Essentially, it is the way in which ideas or information are put to us, which affects how we evaluate them. A good example is an operation. One person is told that there is a 90% chance of success, another is told there is a 10% chance of mortality. Multiple studies suggest that those presented with the success rate are more likely to go ahead with the operation than those presented with the mortality rate. Even though the odds are exactly the same, how the information is framed has a huge impact on which decision we take.

So, it's important to question the framing of information in relation to a decision – how else could it be framed, and would that affect your decision? Ideally, take the time to frame the proposition in two ways. Both the one that highlights negative consequences and the one that highlights positive ones.

Case study – Framing

In a study they were conducting, psychologists Tversky and Kahneman asked participants to decide between two treatments for 600 people who had contracted a fatal disease. Treatment A would result in 400 deaths and 200 lives being saved, and treatment B had a 33% chance that no one would die but a 66% chance that everyone would die.

The options were presented as either positive framing (how many people would live) or negative framing (how many people would die). Treatment A received the most support (72%) when framed as saving 200 lives but dropped significantly (to 22%) when framed as losing 400 lives. This demonstrates that the choices we make are influenced by the way that the options available to us are framed.

See Amos Tversky and Daniel Kahneman, 'The Framing of Decisions and the Psychology of Choice', *Behavioural Decision Making*, 1985, pp. 25–41.

Chapter 3

Building up to the decision point

This chapter looks at gathering information, consulting people and the process to help you make a decision.

Gathering information

The amount of information you need to gather in advance of a decision is largely related to the size and potential impact of the decision. Big decisions probably need more information, smaller ones need less.

I don't want to patronise you by telling you the obvious information you need to collect – and this book isn't about that. Of course you need to know cost, time, resource available, deadlines and so on. My focus here is more on the elements of decision-making that we 'cheat' on, in particular consulting with others, especially staff and volunteers. It's tempting to think that we know what others will say, so it's quicker to just decide. But, ultimately, cutting corners on consultation will often make your decision harder to implement.

Consultation

Consulting before taking a decision is generally accepted as good practice, but far too often, that consultation is 'nonsultation' – in other words, we don't do it properly. It's very common for decision-makers to take a decision, then consult on the decision after they've taken it – and then be surprised when people resist the decision or find all sorts of flaws with it.

It's easy to view consultation as a process which we 'do' to other people, because we vaguely remember being told that's what you're supposed to do. But the key purpose of consultation is to gather information in order to make a better decision. If you consult before you make the decision, you almost don't need to consult afterwards (although, of course, you should probably still ask for people's comments and questions on your decision).

In larger organisations, or those with lots of volunteers, most decisions have to be implemented by people in the farther outreaches of the organisation (i.e. not close to the leadership level). Very few decisions only affect those at the top. So, logically, it makes no sense not to ask those people who will be affected by, and have to implement, the decision what they think the decision should be. You are asking for trouble if you invite people to comment on a decision you have already made!

Even with something as big as a change in strategy, you should ask people what they think the strategy should be in the first place – not their opinion on the strategy you've come up with. And you should do this using proper open questions, and before you've made up your own mind.

There are two main benefits to this approach. Firstly, other people know things you don't, which might affect the ability of the organisation to implement the strategy. Secondly, it involves them fully in the decision-making, which means that when it comes to briefing the decision and implementing it, they're already onside.

If you spend lots of time thinking about strategy or structure and then merely brief your final decision to the staff without having engaged them in the thinking, don't be surprised when you get kickback. You might have been going through the decision-making process in your head for months, but they haven't – give people time to catch up! You can't expect those who have just heard about it to be in the same mental and emotional space as those who have spent ages reflecting on it.

There are two main reasons why people tend to 'cheat' on consultation. Firstly, it's because they think it will slow down decision-making, and secondly, because they think they already know what the answer is. But the reality is that if you want to bring people with you, and have a plurality of voices and opinions, then you have to involve them – even if there's a very good chance that they'll come up with the same decision you have. If folk feel they've been involved in the decision-making (properly involved, not pandered to), then they'll be more invested in making it work.

However, remember to manage expectations. If there is a part of the decision that is non-negotiable and not up for consultation, be clear about that. For example, if you're refurbishing the office but there is a fixed budget, tell folk what the budget is to ensure they won't ask for silk-lined office chairs! If you're not clear about what is and what isn't open for feedback and input, people may end up feeling that the consultation was tokenistic.

The true test of proper consultation is that you don't have to issue a set of FAQs. If you've involved folk from the start, they already know the answers.

Sharing your ideas

I'm a firm advocate of sharing your thinking. It is very rare that what you're considering is genuinely too sensitive to share – especially if you're framing it as questions you're mulling over.

Even if you're thinking about something that might concern specific folk, for example in the case of restructuring, you can ask people questions such as

'How do you think we could organise ourselves better?' or 'Do you think our current structure is working?' to gauge their thoughts.

> **Top tip**
> Don't wait until ideas are fully formed before you start sharing them. Tell people you're just thinking out loud and haven't decided – you just want to test your thinking.

Of course, this is a matter of judgement, as you may find that some of your thoughts concern confidential matters which are too risky to share. However, don't forget that even though you believe there are good reasons not to share your thinking at the beginning, you will still get kickback and resistance if you don't.

If you are worried about sharing your thoughts, really question yourself why that is the case. If you have an open and transparent communication culture within your organisation, then you should have little to fear. And if you don't, a well-run, genuine and open sharing process will help build that culture.

Testing your thinking is equally helpful with something small (like wondering out loud if you ought to organise a staff/trustee get-together) as it is with something big (like investing in a new IT system). When you involve people in the thinking, you either find out all the reasons why it's not a good idea or you get buy-in and commitment to making it work.

> **Top tip**
> Use email chains or social media channels to facilitate ideas and discussion. Pose questions rather than make statements, e.g. 'What flexible working arrangements do you think we should consider?' or 'Do you think our vision statement is still relevant, and if not, how do you think it should change?'

Also bear in mind that it's through testing your thinking that you find out things that might severely disrupt how enthusiastic folk will be in implementing your decision. Something that seems like a very minor thing to you can have a big impact on the success of the decision.

> **Case study – Minor detail, big impact**
> Two large military organisations had to merge, each run by a headquarters containing hundreds of staff. The officer responsible for the merger grappled with a series of complex options around responsibilities, finance, logistics and a myriad of other aspects. But it was only through consultation that they discovered that what mattered most to the staff, and especially those forced to relocate to the receiving headquarters, was how they would get to work. The decisions made on car parking coloured people's whole attitude to what was perceived as a cost-saving merger with little operational impact. Success in the car park led to a successful merger.

Trustees

All of the above is true of trustees as well. We tend to think we have to have a fully formed, costed, worked-out plan before we involve trustees. And then we get all cross and defensive when they point out flaws or otherwise criticise what we've done.

> **Where next?**
> For more on decision-making at board level, see *It's a Battle on the Board*:
>
> www.dsc.org.uk/bob

But trustees are humans just like anyone else. Test your thinking on them first. Involve them in discussions. You don't have to organise formal meetings either. The trick is to ensure that trustees know which decisions are theirs to take (see page 11) and which are best left to the staff.

The process of decision-making

Like with most things, it helps to have a checklist of the decision-making process to go through. This ensures that you don't find yourself facing difficulties further down the line because you missed a stage. And it is also useful when you get to the review stage.

1. Share your thinking right at the start.
2. Ask others who should be involved in the thinking and who might have valuable perspectives to offer.
3. Think about what might help in the decision-making (data, stories, numbers).
4. Decide on a deadline to make your decision.
5. Gather the evidence and information you need to make the decision.
6. Look for evidence which contradicts what you already know.
7. Discuss with folk – up and down the organisation.
8. Moot your early decision, making it clear it's open for change.
9. Get the feedback.
10. Make the changes.
11. Brief.
12. Implement.
13. Check.
14. Amend.

The bit of this process that should take the longest is from 1 to 9. The more time you spend involving people in the early stages, the more likely it is that your decision will stand the test of time. I discuss 11 to 14 in the next chapter.

Three Ps that might get in the way of decision-making

- **Perfection** – wanting things to be perfect. Build resilience to change things as the decision is being implemented.
- **Position** – deciding what you think the decision should be in advance. Better to encourage open mindsets and creativity.
- **Pattern** – doing what is familiar rather than what is new. Don't expect different results if you follow the same route.

Using artificial intelligence in decision-making

We are in the very early days of artificial intelligence (AI), but all the trends indicate that these technologies are gradually becoming part of business as usual for many. Some charities even see AI as an extension of their team, asking these tools to test and challenge ideas.

For example, I know charities that, in order to test ideas, have asked tools such as ChatGPT to write SWOT analyses for them or to play the part of a sceptical team member. Another charity used ChatGPT to analyse staff insights and develop organisational objectives as part of the process of developing a new strategic plan. In all of these cases, the charity has benefitted from having an additional perspective, enabling it to refine ideas rapidly, and reach decisions more quickly and with greater confidence.

While there is huge potential to build charities' capabilities and capacity through AI, we need to be aware of the decisions we are outsourcing to these tools and plan how we might manage the unintended consequences. For instance, when deciding which applicants to choose for an interview, some organisations are using AI to determine if job applications are written by AI. However, these tools can end up flagging candidates who did not use AI but for whom English is not their first language.

There is more guidance about the use of AI in your charity in our AI checklist for charity trustees and leaders (https://zoeamar.com/artificial-intelligence/ai-checklist-for-charity-trustees-and-leaders).

Zoe Amar, Digital Expert

Chapter 4

Implementing the decision

This chapter focuses on the key actions needed to make sure that your decision is implemented in the way you planned.

Brief

Once the decision has finally been made, it needs to be briefed. And this is where it is really important not to take any shortcuts, particularly if it is a key decision that has quite a big impact. You need to think about who needs to know about the decision, including those who might be affected by or interested in it – it's not just those who have to implement the decision.

You should never rely on written briefs alone. A written brief should be the back-up for your face-to-face verbal brief, where people can see and hear you, where you can put enthusiasm into your words, and where everyone can listen to questions being asked and the answers given (which might also prompt some further questions).

Remember that even where the decision has been made at senior level and affects all or large parts of the organisation, it is not always (or even often) down to the senior leaders to do the briefing. It's much more powerful if decisions are briefed through the line – that is, by each team's own line manager, not least because they'll be the ones supporting the implementation of the decision. Senior decision-makers need to brief their leaders face to face and model how to do it so that they can do the same down the line.

To support those briefing the decision, it's a good idea to produce a set of notes for them with the key points, but I would avoid writing their script for them. Using bullet points is better because that gives folk the freedom to be themselves in the briefing, which adds more credibility to the brief.

> ### Briefing notes example
> *Context*
> Reducing staff numbers means moving to a smaller office to save money.
>
> *Key points*
> - Move – 14 Feb
> - Packing up – two days prior to move
> - Desk space diagram
> - One day to orient and sort out work spaces
> - Review of desk allocation in six months

And be absolutely clear that the decision has been made and this is a *briefing*, not a further consultation.

Implement

To be honest, once you've briefed the decision, you are basically implementing it. You've pressed the 'go' button. Now, just let folk get on with delivering it.

But it's important to let people know there's a get-out clause. Folk tend to get more resistant to things that they think they're going to be stuck with. They overthink the consequences. With *most* decisions, it's better to implement them like they're an 'experiment'. Frame it something like: 'We're pretty confident this is the right course of action, but things could change, so we're going to keep an eye on how it's going and do a full review in six months and then change what isn't working.'

That gives folk the psychological headspace to be open to the decision and to continue thinking how it could be done better. It also means they feel less trapped and therefore less resistant to helping to make it work. In my experience, initial discomfort or resistance disappears very quickly, especially if folk know there is a possibility of changing things.

> ### Case study – Adapting to change
>
> I was once implementing a change in an office space. Folk were still in the same office, but we were changing where they sat. This was in order to facilitate better working between teams.
>
> Quite a few of the people involved were very resistant to moving their desk space, as they were attached to where they sat. However, once I had framed it like an experiment – 'we're going to try this for a bit and in a few months, if it isn't achieving what we hoped, we'll change it back' – folk became more willing to go with the change. Reluctantly, I must admit, but they did move.
>
> Within two weeks of the move, they were all perfectly happy with the new space they were in. People will adapt, but you have to be persistent, give them a get-out option and offer a timeline. And insist they give it a go.

Check

All decisions require you to make sure they are working and to find out what extra help might be needed. You need to check in on folk to make sure that they have the right understanding, tools and resources to make the decision work. And you need to get feedback on how it's going and to look at evidence of the effectiveness of the decision.

Checking in can be both informal (such as a catch-up at a one-to-one) and formal (such as a session during a meeting). With really big decisions, you might even have a project plan or Gantt chart that tracks progress, but often you find out much more by having conversations rather than looking at spreadsheets, which can never tell you the whole story. Chapter 5 has more on how to follow up on and evaluate your decisions.

Amend

Once you've made a decision, it's tempting to stick at it at all costs. There are many reasons for this: you may think it was the right one and to change it feels like implying lack of confidence in your own judgement or that you've failed in some way; or you might think that changing it will imply you're weak.

However, what matters is that the decision works – and if by changing something you can get a better outcome, then why wouldn't you? Very few decisions are perfect when you come up with them. There's an old military saying, attributed to Helmuth von Moltke, that 'no plan survives contact with the enemy'. And that's true of decisions. Once you're implementing a decision, things are bound to crop up that you either hadn't thought of or thought would be easy to overcome (and it turns out they're not).

It's a sign of strength to change or amend a decision, but there are still rules and things you need to think about before you do it. Consider:

- Do you really need to change the decision? Perhaps you simply have reached a difficult patch and need to navigate it. Or maybe folk need to be reminded of and reconnected to the context of, the reason for and the aim of the decision.
- What are the consequences of making this amendment?
- Who needs to know about the change?
- Is it a short-term fix that might cause problems in the longer term?

Notwithstanding all that, always be open to making a change. At the end of the day, it's not the decision itself that matters but what it's intended to achieve.

Chapter 5

Following up

This chapter looks at quick and easy ways to assess how good your decision was.

Why evaluate?

You make a decision, you implement it, it works, you move on to the next thing. That's how life works, of course. But you really miss a trick when you fail to remind yourself of decisions that have been successful. When you remind people of the situation you were in, what you decided to do and what happened, it reinforces trust in the process, it helps them to feel good about being part of things moving forward and, most of all, it reminds them that more often than not the organisation is making good decisions.

Sharing successful outcomes at regular briefings is important. It's also always worth doing a Plus/Delta evaluation. The 'plus' bit is where you look at what went well and the 'delta' bit (delta being a common mathematical term for a change in something) is where you look at what you could have done differently or would change in the future.

> **Where next?**
> Get in touch with DSC's in-house training team for courses on problem-solving and decision-making:
>
> www.dsc.org.uk/in-house-training-2

Evaluate

One of the easiest ways to approach evaluation is by simply gathering folk together and asking straightforward, open questions about both the decision-making process and the outcome of the decision.

Decision-making process

Go back to your original process checklist (see page 24) and assess how you did against each of the stages. Did you skip any part of the process? Did you skimp on one part because you were too busy or it felt like too much of an effort? Ask those involved:

- What worked in how you came up with the decision?
- What should you change for the future?
- What worked well about the way you gathered the information?
- What information did you miss?
- What could you do in the future to make sure you have all the information necessary?
- Is there anything that could have been improved in the way the decision was communicated?
- What would have helped people to understand the decision better?
- What could you do in the future to make people feel more engaged in, or committed to, delivering the decision?

Feedback like this gives you valuable information to make sure you've got everyone onside for any future decisions you are making.

The outcome of the decision

With the decision itself, think about what drove that decision in the first place – did anything change along the way that meant that the decision had to change?

Ask folk the following:

- What have we achieved with this decision?
- What haven't we achieved?
- What would have made it a better decision?
- What do we need to change now?
- What do we need to change for the future?

Such feedback will help you to know if your decision was a good one – that is, whether the outcome the decision was meant to achieve was delivered or only parts of it were. That gives you the opportunity to establish why it went well or what could be done differently for the future. It also allows you to see what needs to change now to get the outcome you want.

Above all, communicate what you have learned. Tell folk what went well and what went less well, what you have learned and what you plan for the future. That way people get used to constant feedback, to not associating change with failure and to being open to learning.

Remember

None of us set out to make a bad decision – it is only ever bad in hindsight. But where a decision didn't achieve what you hoped it would, going back and reviewing your processes will help you to understand where it might have gone wrong.

Be brave, be bold, be decisive. And be prepared to change your mind!